Incident Management

A Guide to IT Incident Management

Fabrizio Zuccari

"La gestione di un incidente deve prevedere sia gli aspetti utili a prevenire che tali eventualità accadano, sia le misure per reagire in modo corretto e pianificato per ripristinare nella maniera più efficace i livelli di servizio compromessi."
(Francesco La Trofa - Giornalista e divulgatore tecnologico)

"Incident management must encompass both the aspects aimed at preventing such eventualities from occurring, as well as measures to react in a correct and planned way to restore compromised service levels most effectively."
(Francesco La Trofa - Journalist and Technology Communicator)

Table of Contents

Introduction to Incident Management

Initially, it is critical to clarify the nature and importance of incident management within the broader context of IT service management.

The Incident Management area focuses on the timely and efficient management of events that can compromise the continuity and quality of the IT services provided to the organization.

Disruptions and anomalies, if not addressed promptly and effectively, can lead to serious consequences, including significant operational disruptions, financial losses, and negative reputational impacts, so incident management is a critical tool in ensuring the stability and reliability of IT services, as well as ensuring that the organization is able to respond adequately and professionally to unforeseen challenges that may arise emerge.

To fully understand incident management and implement it successfully, it is essential to explore the established frameworks and methodologies that provide guidelines and best practices in this field. Among these, two of the most well-known and widely adopted stand out: ITIL (**I**nformation **T**echnology **I**nfrastructure **L**ibrary**)** and COBIT **(C**ontrol **Ob**jectives for **I**nformation and Related **T**echnologies): these frameworks offer a series of processes, procedures and tools designed specifically to support effective incident management, providing IT operators with a structured and unified framework to successfully address emerging challenges.

Definition and objectives of Incident Management

The incident management process has a set of well-defined objectives.

Among them, there is the importance of timely and accurate recording of events, which allows you to create a detailed archive of all relevant information. This data includes the time of occurrence, the functional areas affected, a precise description of the symptoms encountered, and any other information that may facilitate subsequent analysis and resolution.

This repository provides the foundation for analyzing and developing solutions, improving the organization's ability to proactively respond to similar future events.

Another important aspect is represented by root cause analysis, which aims to identify not only the visible symptoms of the incident, but the real causes that generated it. This preventive approach makes it possible to prevent the same incidents from happening again, correcting structural problems that may have occurred in systems or processes. Root cause analysis can include techniques such as collecting and analyzing historical data, questioning stakeholders involved, and identifying vulnerabilities at a technological or procedural level.

A further step is the classification and prioritization of incidents according to their severity and urgency.

This allows resources to be allocated efficiently, devoting more attention to critical incidents that could have a significant impact on the business.

Prioritization can be supported by standardized frameworks that offer objective methodologies to determine the urgency and severity of each incident. Through proper classification, the organization can better manage its workflow, balancing urgent interventions with those that require a more complex resolution.

Timely resolution is one of the most important aspects of incident management. The speed with which an incident is resolved is directly proportional to the organization's ability to restore operational normality and reduce the impact on business operations. However, the speed of resolution must not compromise the quality of the solutions adopted. In some cases, workarounds may need to be implemented to immediately mitigate the impact of an incident, especially when the final resolution requires more time or resources. These workarounds allow you to maintain continuity of service, while waiting for a permanent solution that eliminates the problem at the root.

Additionally, transparent and proactive communication with end-users is crucial for maintaining trust in the system. During incident management, affected users must be constantly updated on the progress of the resolution, the nature of the problem and the expected timeline for restoring service. Optimal communication management not only increases user satisfaction, but also helps prevent misunderstandings or misaligned expectations.

A further aspect of incident management is continuous improvement: in addition to resolving incidents, post-mortem analysis of each critical event gives the organization the opportunity to learn from mistakes and optimize its processes.

This continuous feedback loop allows you to hone your incident management capabilities, improving not only the speed and effectiveness of future responses, but also the overall resilience of your IT systems.

The adoption of key performance indicators (KPIs) allows you to monitor the performance of the incident management process over time, highlighting areas for improvement and supporting strategic decisions.

Implementing preventative solutions such as process automation and the integration of proactive monitoring systems can greatly reduce the number and severity of incidents. Not only does this help you react to events faster and more efficiently, but you also create a more robust IT environment that is less prone to disruption.

Incident Management and IT Service Management

The differences between incident management and IT service management (ITSM) are outlined through a reflection on two distinct but complementary concepts within the context of Information Technology (IT): incident management focuses on the timely resolution of negative events affecting IT services, while ITSM embraces a broader approach that covers the entire lifecycle of IT services. from design to supply and continuous improvement, in order to meet business needs.
Incident management, therefore, is configured as a specific and immediate component within ITSM, dedicated to the management of unexpected events and service interruptions. Its primary objective is to restore normal IT services to normal operations in the shortest possible time, thus minimizing the negative impact on business operations and end-user satisfaction.

On the other hand, ITSM embraces a more holistic and

strategic approach to IT service management, considering the entire lifecycle of services, from their conception to their retirement. This approach focuses on designing IT services that meet the needs and goals of the organization, transitioning them smoothly into the operating environment, providing the services efficiently and reliably, and continuously improving to adapt to business changes and technological evolutions.

While incident management is primarily concerned with reactive and unforeseen events, ITSM also incorporates a proactive dimension through the planning and implementation of processes and procedures to prevent future incidents and constantly improve the reliability and quality of IT services.

This includes implementing practices such as problem management and change management, which aim to identify and address the underlying causes of recurring incidents and ensure that changes in the IT environment are managed in a controlled and secure manner.

Overview of ITIL and COBIT frameworks

An exhaustive analysis of the preeminent frameworks in the context of IT service and incident management reveals the importance and relevance of ITIL (Information Technology Infrastructure Library) and COBIT (Control Objectives for Information and Related Technologies).

ITIL emerges as a well-established body of *best practices*, outlining comprehensive approaches for designing, delivering, and continuously improving IT services.
In contrast, COBIT stands out for its focus on aligning business goals with IT operations, orchestrating control and governance over processes.

ITIL, as an emblem of standardization in the IT sector, offers a broad overview of the processes necessary to ensure IT service excellence: this framework, developed by the CCTA of the British Government (**C**entral **C**omputer and **T**elecommunications **A**gency), now OGC (**O**ffice of **G**overnment **C**ommerce), is structured around a series of books that deal with various aspects of IT service management.

Through its structure, ITIL clearly outlines the processes to be adopted for incident management, including best practices for incident recording, classification, resolution and continuous monitoring.

COBIT focuses on the synergy between business objectives and IT activities, providing a framework to ensure that IT contributes in a consistent and aligned way to the overall success of the organization: originally developed by the ISACA (**I**nformation **S**ystems **A**udit and **C**ontrol **A**ssociation) it provides a set of control objectives that link business objectives to IT management activities.
This framework provides valuable guidance for establishing controls and processes that ensure the security, reliability, and effectiveness of IT operations.

Both frameworks, in addition to providing in-depth guidelines for IT service management, also include specific provisions for effective incident management: ITIL, for example, devotes an entire book to service desk operations, which covers processes related to incident management in detail, while COBIT integrates incident management within the service and application delivery domain (DS), providing a framework for controlling and monitoring incident-related activities.

Preparation and Prevention

Preparedness and prevention are key actions to ensure an effective and timely response to unforeseen events. We examine in more detail the importance of preparedness and preventive measures in incident management through an analysis of the strategies and practices needed to mitigate the risk of incidents and ensure business continuity in dynamic environments.

The provision of resources, processes and personnel to deal

with potential adverse events is the first step in incident management: it involves the creation and maintenance of emergency plans and standard operating procedures, as well as the training and preparation of personnel to deal with critical situations.

Preparation also includes clearly defining roles and responsibilities within the organization when managing incidents, ensuring efficient resource allocation and effective coordination of activities.

Prevention also plays an equally important role in reducing the risk of incidents: this includes proactively identifying and analyzing potential sources of risk within the IT environment, as well as implementing countermeasures and preventive controls to mitigate those risks. It can take many forms, including implementing robust cybersecurity policies, conducting periodic vulnerability and risk analyses, and adopting advanced technologies for detecting and preventing cyber threats.

Other aspects to consider are warning signs, which are early indicators of potential problems or serious threats to business continuity, which allow IT operators to intervene preemptively to avoid the occurrence of critical events.

Incident Logging

Accurate incident logging is the starting point for a number of mission-critical tasks, enabling organizations to appropriately monitor, analyze, and respond to service disruptions.

With detailed and timely incident logging, organizations are able to accurately track the magnitude and frequency of anomalies, as well as identify recurring trends that could indicate systematic issues or emerging issues.

A primary aspect of incident recording is the definition of a clear and standardized process that ensures consistency and uniformity in the documentation of the various situations: this process should be designed to capture a series of crucial information including:

- The date and time of the incident,
- A detailed description of the problem encountered,
- The level of severity of the incident
- The parties involved or the affected users.

This data forms the basis for an in-depth analysis of the underlying causes of incidents and for the identification of opportunities for improvement of the processes or IT systems involved.

Accurate incident logging enables organizations to meet regulatory compliance requirements and account for their incident management performance: Maintaining a detailed record of incidents is often required by industry regulations and standards, such as ISO 20000 for IT service management.

In this context, comprehensive and accurate documentation of incidents not only helps organizations meet regulatory obligations, but also demonstrate a commitment to transparency and operational excellence.

Finally, incident logging provides an empirical basis for continuous improvement of IT processes and services.

By analyzing the data collected through incident logging, companies can identify areas of weakness or inefficiency in their systems and processes, and implement targeted corrective actions to mitigate risks and improve the overall quality of the services provided.

In this way, incident logging becomes a valuable means of optimizing IT operations and ensuring greater reliability and end-user satisfaction.

Identifying Warning Signs

Identifying warning signs allows you to anticipate and prevent the occurrence of critical and prolonged events that could compromise business continuity and user satisfaction. These signals, manifesting themselves in various ways, are valuable indications of potential problems or anomalies in IT systems and services, requiring immediate attention and timely response to avoid unintended consequences.

The warning signs can take many forms, reflecting the complexity and diversity of challenges that can emerge in the IT environment.
Among these, anomalies in the system's monitoring data stand out (**e.g.:** *significant changes in performance levels, increased errors or response times, or decreased availability of services*).

Proactive monitoring of key performance parameters and continuous analysis of monitoring data enable these warning signs to be detected early and preventive corrective actions to be taken to mitigate the risk of incidents.

User reports are another important source of warning signs,

as end users are often the first to experience problems or anomalies in the use of IT services.

To effectively detect warning signs, it is essential to establish proactive monitoring mechanisms and well-structured user feedback processes. This may include implementing automated monitoring tools that alert IT staff to abnormal changes in system parameters, as well as establishing formal procedures for handling user reports and classifying them based on severity and urgency. Fostering a company culture that encourages users to report problems early and accurately can significantly contribute to the early identification of warning signs and the prevention of incidents.

Implementation of preventive measures

The implementation of preventive measures is one of the focal elements in the incident management strategy, as it aims to reduce the likelihood of unwanted events occurring and mitigate their impact on business operations.

These preventive measures, taken proactively, are configured as a first layer of security and business continuity of the organization, providing a first layer of defense against potential threats and vulnerabilities in the

IT context.

Among the most relevant and commonly adopted preventive measures, the implementation of regular security patches stands out: patches represent software updates designed to fix known vulnerabilities and security flaws in operating systems, applications and IT devices. Careful planning and timely application of these patches help keep systems up-to-date and reduce the attack surface for potential cyber threats, thereby improving the overall resilience of the IT system.

Regular verification and updating of data backup and recovery processes is another essential preventive measure to ensure business continuity in the event of incidents such as data loss or corruption: a robust and well-planned backup strategy, including regular full and incremental backups, as well as data retention in secure and remote recovery sites, It significantly reduces the risk of critical data loss and enables fast and effective recovery when needed.

In parallel, training personnel to deal with emergency situations effectively plays an equally important role in preventing incidents: well-trained personnel are able to recognize early signs of potential problems, respond promptly to emerging threats, and take appropriate actions to limit the impact of incidents on business operations. This training should be targeted and continuous, integrating emergency simulations, hands-on training sessions, and regular updates on standard operating procedures.

Finally, it is crucial that preventive measures are integrated into the company culture and constantly monitored to ensure their effectiveness in preventing future incidents. This requires an ongoing commitment from business leadership to inculcate a proactive mindset toward security and risk management across all departments and levels of the organization. In addition, regular security and effectiveness assessments of the preventive measures implemented should be conducted in order to identify any gaps or areas for improvement and to make the necessary adjustments to ensure maximum protection and resilience of the corporate IT environment.

Detection and Reporting

Early detection and reporting are essential for effective management of unwanted events.

We delve into the vital importance of early incident detection, examining the implementation of effective reporting systems and emphasizing the crucial role of personnel in the act of reporting incidents.

In a dynamic and complex IT environment, the ability to promptly spot signs of anomalies or deviations from normal operations is a critical skill to mitigate the potential negative impact on users and business operations.

Through early identification of incidents, organizations can intervene early to limit the spread of adverse effects and initiate targeted corrective actions to restore normal operations.

In parallel with detection, incident reporting plays a crucial role in ensuring an effective response to unwanted events. Effective reporting systems provide a formal and structured channel through which staff can quickly and accurately communicate the onset of an incident to the team responsible for managing it.

These systems should be designed to allow for the rapid transmission of relevant information, including details about the incident, its impact on operations, and the immediate actions taken to address it.

The success of reporting systems also depends to a large extent on the commitment and awareness of personnel in identifying and reporting incidents: the role of personnel is crucial not only in recognizing signs of anomalies or malfunctions, but also in taking a proactive attitude towards the reporting of such critical events.

Fostering a corporate culture that values and rewards incident reporting, encouraging transparency and openness in addressing challenges, is essential to ensure a constant and reliable flow of information on any issues encountered.

Incident detection processes

Incident detection processes aim to detect anomalies or outages in the organization's systems and networks early and accurately.

These processes are designed to ensure constant monitoring and prompt responsiveness in the face of any deviations from normal operations.

Among the most commonly used methods in incident detection processes is the continuous monitoring of the performance of systems and networks: through the use of dedicated tools and the constant analysis of key performance parameters, companies are able to quickly identify significant changes that could indicate the presence of problems or anomalies. This proactive monitoring allows you to detect potential threats before they can cause significant damage, allowing for an immediate and targeted response.

In addition to performance monitoring, analyzing event logs is another essential tactic for incident detection.

Event logs, or log files, are detailed records of all activities and events that occur in systems and networks.

Through a systematic analysis of these logs, organizations can spot warning signs and abnormal patterns that could indicate the presence of ongoing or upcoming incidents. However, it is important that this analysis is conducted with criterion and competence, as the amount of data generated can be vast and complex.

Finally, implementing automated anomaly detection systems is an advanced and proactive approach to incident detection. These systems use AI algorithms and models to identify irregular patterns or anomalous behavior in system data, allowing for early detection of potential threats or malfunctions. However, it is critical that such systems are accurately configured and calibrated to minimize false positives and ensure a reliable and efficient response.

As part of your incident detection processes, it is essential to establish clear and well-defined criteria for anomaly detection, as well as to ensure that your processes are able to identify any issues early in order to minimize the impact on business operations.

A systemic, integrated approach to incident detection, leveraging a combination of performance monitoring, log analysis, and automated anomaly detection systems, is the foundation for effective incident management in IT services, ensuring business continuity and security of the organization's digital assets.

Signaling and communication systems

Reporting and communication systems provide essential channels through which users and IT staff can report and communicate promptly about unwanted events and their resolutions.

These systems are designed to facilitate smooth and efficient communication throughout the incident lifecycle, ensuring a prompt and well-coordinated response to mitigate the negative impact on business operations.

One of the key elements of reporting and communication systems is self-service incident reporting portals: these portals provide users with a direct and intuitive means of reporting issues and support requests, allowing them to enter detailed information about the incident and monitor the progress of its resolution.

The ease of use and accessibility of such portals are of paramount importance, as they encourage quick and accurate incident reporting by users, minimizing downtime and improving overall user satisfaction.

In addition to self-service portals, dedicated telephone lines are another important communication channel for incident reporting. These lines provide an immediate option for users who prefer to communicate their issues verbally, allowing them to get in direct contact with the IT staff responsible for resolving incidents. It is essential that these lines are handled efficiently and that the support staff is properly trained to handle calls in a professional and decisive manner.

In addition to self-service portals and phone lines, ticketing systems or incident management software are a key component of reporting and communication systems: these systems allow IT staff to record, track, and manage user-reported incidents in an organized manner, ensuring a systematic and well-documented response to each report. Through the use of such systems, you can monitor the progress of incident resolution, assign tasks and responsibilities effectively, and generate detailed reports on the overall performance of your IT team.

It is important that reporting systems are designed to ensure that information is transmitted quickly and accurately to IT personnel responsible for incident management: this requires proper configuration and optimization of communication channels, as well as the establishment of clear and well-structured procedures for routing and prioritizing incident reports.

Only through the implementation of robust and well-integrated reporting and communication systems can organizations ensure timely and effective response to incidents while maintaining high standards of service and user satisfaction.

Role of staff in reporting

The role of personnel in incident reporting is a key element in the early detection and timely resolution of problems or anomalies.

We look in more detail at the critical role of staff in incident reporting, highlighting the importance of awareness, training, and collaboration to ensure efficient management of unwanted events.

The first crucial aspect concerns staff awareness of incident warning signs: it is essential that staff are educated and aware of symptoms and indications that could suggest the presence of an incident, such as anomalies in system performance, recurring errors or user reports. Through accurate awareness, staff will be able to promptly recognize and report any anomalies, thus contributing to early detection of incidents and timely response.

It is of paramount importance to provide staff with the

necessary training on how to correctly report problems or anomalies: this includes not only working knowledge of the processes and tools used for incident reporting, but also an understanding of the protocols and procedures that must be followed to ensure accurate and detailed communication of relevant information. Proper training ensures that staff are able to report incidents effectively and consistently, thereby improving the timeliness and accuracy of responses.

The active involvement of staff in incident reporting plays an important role in ensuring efficient and timely incident management: when staff are motivated and empowered in incident reporting, an environment is created where collaboration and effective communication become the norm.

This promotes greater transparency and information sharing between IT staff and end users, allowing for a coordinated and well-informed response to unwanted events.

Collaboration and effective communication between IT staff and end users remain key elements for effective and timely incident management: when staff and end users work together to report and resolve incidents, it creates an environment where information is exchanged quickly and accurately, allowing for a prompt and well-coordinated response to critical events. Through strong collaboration and communication, you can maximize the reliability and availability of your company's IT services while ensuring higher end-user satisfaction.

Classification and Initial Support

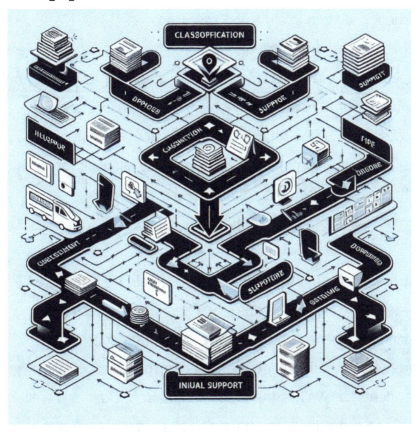

The initial classification and support process plays a primary role in determining the nature and magnitude of events, thus ensuring an adequate and timely response.

Let's explore in more depth the criteria used for incident classification, strategies for prioritization, and the essential role in providing initial support and response to affected users.

The incident classification process is based on well-defined and standardized criteria, which allow the severity and urgency of each event to be assessed.

These criteria may include assessing the impact on business operations, the technical complexity involved, as well as the criticality of the services involved. Through accurate assessment based on these criteria, each incident can be assigned an appropriate level of priority, allowing for efficient resource management and a response proportionate to its severity.

Strategies for incident prioritization should be considered in order to maximize the efficiency and effectiveness of the response: these strategies may include the adoption of predefined models or frameworks for the classification of incidents, as well as the implementation of clear and well-defined procedures for managing the different priority levels. Through proper prioritization, it is possible to ensure that the most critical and urgent incidents are dealt with as promptly and carefully as possible, while the smaller ones can be handled in a more flexible and gradual manner.

Providing initial support and response to affected users plays a vital role in the incident management process: initial support personnel must be adequately trained and equipped with the necessary skills to deal with a wide range of situations, providing timely and professional assistance to users affected by incidents.

This can include resolving immediate technical issues, providing relevant information and instructions, as well as managing user expectations during the resolution process.

Criteria for Classification of Incidents

The criteria for classifying incidents are varied, reflecting the complexity of the challenges faced within IT operations. One of the main criteria adopted is the complexity of the problem itself, which can be assessed based on its technical nature, its spread over several systems or the extent of the resources involved.

Understanding complexity allows you to establish a clear picture of the extent of the incident, thus facilitating its management and resolution.

In addition, the number of affected users is another important criterion for the classification of incidents. An incident involving a large number of users can have a significant impact on business operations, requiring an immediate and prioritized response. Therefore, assessing the size of the impact on users is crucial to determine the severity of the incident and prioritize its management.

Similarly, the impact on business productivity is a crucial criterion in the classification of incidents: events that cause prolonged interruptions or significant data loss can seriously compromise business operations, thus requiring timely and targeted intervention to mitigate the damage. Productivity impact assessment allows you to focus resources where they are needed most, ensuring effective incident response.

The criticality of the affected services also plays a critical role in the classification of incidents: events that compromise the availability or reliability of services critical to business operations must be handled with the utmost urgency and care.
Assessing the criticality of the services involved is of primary importance in determining the priority and commitment needed to resolve incidents.

Incident prioritization

After the classification phase, the incident management process continues with prioritization – a critical step in allocating resources efficiently and ensuring that critical issues are addressed as quickly as possible.

Incident prioritisation is based on a careful assessment of the seriousness and urgency of each event, adopting specific criteria that allow an order of intervention to be established.

The prioritization criteria are different and are selected according to the complexity of the situations and the specific needs of the organization: one of the main criteria adopted is the level of impact of incidents on business operations.

Incidents that cause major disruptions or compromise the continuity of critical processes will be prioritized, as they require immediate and complete resolution to minimize the negative impact on the business.

The time it takes to resolve the incident can also be a determining criterion in prioritization: incidents that require a quick resolution to limit damage and restore normal operations will be treated with higher priority than those that can be handled more flexibly over time.

The criticality of the affected services is an additional prioritization criterion, as incidents that affect services vital to business operations will be treated with greater urgency than those involving less critical services.

It is crucial to establish a clear and transparent process for prioritizing incidents in order to ensure a quick and effective response.

This process should be supported by well-defined guidelines and communicated effectively to all personnel involved in incident management.

It is important that the process includes monitoring and review mechanisms to ensure that incidents are addressed in accordance with established priorities and that any deviations are corrected promptly: only through a structured and well-managed approach to incident prioritization can effective and efficient management of critical situations be ensured.

Provide initial support and response

The phase of providing the first support and the initial response is the starting point for effectively addressing and resolving critical situations.

This phase not only represents the first point of contact between the organization and the affected user, but also directly affects how the incident will be perceived and addressed. Carefully reviewing the steps involved in this phase allows you to outline best practices for providing effective care, minimizing the impact on business operations and improving post-critical recovery.

- **Reassurance of affected users**:

  One of the key aspects of the initial response is the ability to communicate with users in a timely manner, reassuring them that the incident has been taken care of. Reassurance plays a fundamental psychological role, as it allows you to contain users' anxiety and uncertainty. This step must be done quickly, using clear and professional language to convey the seriousness with which the incident is handled.

  E.g.: *Automatically sending acknowledgements of receipt of the report through a ticket management system can be an essential first step. This approach builds trust and shows that the incident management process is well underway and structured.*

  Timely communication can include information such as the number of reference tickets and a preliminary estimate of response times. This transparency not only reduces the workload of support teams, avoiding repeated requests for updates, but also improves the overall user experience. This avoids the risk of uncertainty turning into frustration, which could negatively affect the perception of the service offered by the organization.

- **Provide preliminary mitigation instructions**: Another critical component of the initial response is providing users with immediate instructions to mitigate the effects of the incident. These instructions must be simple, actionable and context-specific, in order to prevent the user from unintentionally worsening the situation. In many cases, the user may be able to take temporary measures to reduce the impact of the incident, thereby reducing the pressure on resolution teams. *E.g.: In the event of an interruption of an online service, guidance can be provided on temporary alternatives or how to avoid operations that could further compromise the system. In the event of a cybersecurity incident, quick user intervention, such as changing passwords or disconnecting from compromised networks, can be crucial to limit the damage.*

This phase therefore requires clear, timely and well-coordinated communication, based on predefined procedures that take into account the different critical scenarios.

- **Effective communication with resolution teams**:

  Managing a critical incident inevitably involves collaboration between different teams within the organization, each with specific expertise. Accurate and timely transfer of information gathered during the initial support phase is crucial to enable resolution teams to operate efficiently. The information submitted must include not only the technical details of the incident, but also a detailed account of the actions already taken, any symptoms detected, and any feedback received from users.

  E.g.: A practical example can be seen in the management of cyberattacks. In such contexts, information regarding the manner of the attack, potential entry points, and compromised data must be communicated quickly and comprehensively to security teams. Only clear and structured communication allows a thorough investigation to begin immediately and the first containment measures to be taken.

- **Staff training and preparation**:

  The success of the initial response phase depends to

a large extent on the preparation of the personnel involved. Proper training is not limited to technical competence alone, but also includes the ability to handle crisis situations with a calm and professional approach. Staff must be able to quickly understand the nature of the incident and know how to effectively interact with both affected users and resolution teams. In high-pressure contexts, such as managing cyber emergencies or critical failures of business systems, support personnel must possess not only technical skills, but also a solid preparation to communicate clearly. This is particularly important in the case of direct interactions with users, where the ability to reassure and provide practical guidance can have a significant impact on the overall management of the crisis.

E.g.: A significant example is the case of customer service agents who have to handle emergency calls: here, the ability to remain calm and provide precise instructions can make the difference between containing or escalating the incident.

Analysis and Diagnosis

In this chapter, the importance of conducting an in-depth analysis of incidents will be examined, not only to effectively solve immediate problems, but more importantly to understand the root causes that originated them.
This understanding is a key element for the prevention of future events and for the continuous improvement of operational processes.
To support this analysis, the fundamental role of diagnostic

tools will be explored, the use of which allows accurate and detailed evaluations to be conducted. The need to involve specialized teams will be highlighted, capable of dealing with complex situations that require specific skills and high technical experience.

- **In-depth analysis of the causes of incident**: Identifying the root causes of an incident requires a rigorous and methodical approach, taking into account not only the surface dynamics of the event, but also the underlying factors that made it possible. This process, often referred to as "*Root Cause Analysis*" (RCA), represents a critical phase in incident management, as it allows you not only to immediately solve the problem, but to identify the conditions that led to the incident, both technical and organizational.

  In the context of a web application experiencing a service outage, for example, a thorough analysis may not be limited to reviewing the source code or hosting infrastructure. It might include a detailed examination of user-system interactions, network configurations, workload management, and update and maintenance policies.

  This multidimensional analysis allows you to identify any flaws in the system, such as human error, unforeseen security vulnerabilities, or inefficiencies in the software testing and deployment processes. The ultimate goal is to prevent the recurrence of the incident and improve the overall reliability of the system.

- **Using diagnostic tools**:

  To conduct effective and detailed root cause analysis, diagnostic tools are an indispensable resource.

  These tools allow you to collect, analyze, and visualize large volumes of data related to system operation and infrastructure performance. Real-time monitoring, log analysis, and network tracking are some of the key features offered by these tools, providing essential information to understand the sequence of events leading up to the incident.

  *E.g.: Tools such as **Splunk** or **ELK Stack** offer advanced solutions for log analysis, allowing you to identify recurring patterns or anomalies that could indicate systemic issues or external attacks. The use of these tools allows you to trace the root causes of incidents with greater accuracy, accelerating response times and improving the quality of the solutions implemented.*

Many diagnostic tools integrate machine learning and artificial intelligence capabilities to automatically detect anomalies or suspicious behavior, making it easy to proactively intervene on potential issues before they turn into full-blown incidents.

- **Involvement of specialized teams**:
  In the case of complex or particularly serious incidents, the involvement of specialized teams becomes an essential element to ensure an effective and timely resolution. These teams, made up of experts with specific skills, are able to address issues that require a high level of specialization, such as cybersecurity incidents, large-scale network issues, or critical software malfunctions

  E.g.: When faced with a complex and evolving threat, such as a ransomware attack or a sophisticated intrusion into corporate systems, a Computer Security Incident Response Team (CSIRT) can take action to identify the source of the attack, isolate compromised areas, mitigate damage, and restore the security of systems. These teams, in addition to possessing advanced technical skills, must have a thorough understanding of cyber defense strategies, security regulations, and best practices for post-incident recovery.

Cooperation between different teams within an organization, from IT technicians to legal and communications experts, is critical to successfully managing complex incidents. Only a coordinated and multidisciplinary approach makes it possible to face the challenges posed by situations that put business continuity and corporate reputation at risk.

Incident analysis techniques

Incident analysis techniques are essential tools for exploring the complex dynamics that lead to critical events, thus offering guidance for taking corrective measures to prevent their recurrence. The effectiveness of such methodologies lies in their ability to thoroughly analyze the technical and organizational variables involved, as well as the interactions that can lead to incidents. Through a systematic and multidisciplinary approach, these techniques make it possible to develop a holistic understanding of incidents and to define mitigation strategies.

Common practices include Root Causes (RCA) analysis, flowcharts, trend analysis, and benchmarking. Each of these methodologies helps to unravel different aspects of the dynamics of incidents, offering a complete view of critical issues and possible interventions.

Root Causes Analysis:

It represents one of the most consolidated and structured methodologies for dealing with complex incidents. This approach focuses on identifying the root causes that generated the incident, trying to go beyond the immediate and superficial manifestations. The RCA is based on a detailed analysis that considers both technical and organizational factors, allowing latent vulnerabilities to be revealed that may not be immediately apparent.

Flowcharts:

They are visual tools that facilitate the analysis of incidents, allowing you to map the sequences of events that led to a given incident. These diagrams clearly and intuitively represent the cause-and-effect relationships between the different actions or steps in the process. Their effectiveness lies in the ability to break down complex situations into simpler steps, making the interactions between variables that might otherwise escape analysis evident.

- **Trend analysis:**

It aims to examine historical incident data in order to identify recurring patterns or behaviors that could suggest areas of vulnerability. This approach is based on the collection and interpretation of a wide range of data, ranging from the number of incidents that occurred in a given period of time, to the frequency and severity of such events. The goal is to anticipate the possibility of future incidents through a preventive analysis oriented towards continuous improvement.

- **The comparative analysis**:
  It is a methodology that is based on the examination of similar incidents that have occurred in related contexts or sectors, in order to draw lessons from past experiences and adopt best practices. This approach provides an important external perspective, as it allows you to compare your own incident management with that of other organizations, identifying potential areas for improvement and innovative solutions.

Diagnostic tools

Diagnostic tools allow you to collect and analyze relevant data and information to fully understand the dynamics underlying undesirable events.

These tools, characterized by a variety of functionalities and capabilities, play an important role in identifying patterns, anomalies and correlations that can be essential for identifying the causes of incidents and devising appropriate solutions.

Performance monitoring software plays a major role in the arsenal of diagnostic tools: this software allows analysts to constantly monitor the performance of IT systems and infrastructures, detecting any changes or anomalies that could indicate the presence of an ongoing incident or a potential imminent risk.
By analyzing performance metrics and identifying significant deviations from normal parameters, these tools provide valuable support for the timely identification and mitigation of incidents.

System event logs are an essential source of information for analysts during the incident diagnosis process: these logs record a wide range of events and activities that occur in IT systems, allowing analysts to reconstruct the context of unwanted events and identify any correlations or sequences of actions that may have contributed to the manifestation of the incident.
Through detailed analysis of system logs, analysts can identify the root causes of incidents and develop

appropriate solutions to mitigate their effects.

Additionally, log analysis tools play a crucial role in the incident diagnosis process, allowing analysts to effectively review and interpret the vast amounts of data contained in system logs.

These tools provide advanced capabilities to filter, view, and analyze system logs, allowing analysts to quickly spot patterns, trends, and anomalies that may be indicative of a potential security incident or issue. Through the use of sophisticated log analysis tools, analysts can gain an in-depth understanding of unwanted events and develop targeted solutions to mitigate the associated risks.

Network traffic monitoring tools allow analysts to observe and analyze the flow of data within corporate networks, identifying any anomalies or suspicious activity that could indicate the presence of a security incident or network issue. Through network traffic analysis, analysts can identify anomalous behavior, identify potential security threats, and implement corrective measures to protect the integrity and security of corporate networks.

Involvement of specialized teams

In the context of incident management, dealing with highly

complex situations often requires the involvement of specialized teams, composed of professionals with specific skills and a deep knowledge of the system involved. These teams, which can be made up of cybersecurity experts, network engineers, software developers, or operating system experts, are a valuable resource for successfully dealing with the most intricate and delicate incidents. Involving these teams allows you to make the most of the specialized knowledge and skills needed to fully understand the nature of the incident and develop targeted, customized solutions to resolve it.

- **Cybersecurity experts:**
  They play a crucial role in protecting the integrity of business systems.
  In an age where cyber threats are constantly evolving, their presence is essential to identify, mitigate, and prevent security breaches. These professionals are trained to detect vulnerabilities that could be exploited by external or internal attacks and conduct thorough investigations to understand the nature of the incident. Their expertise includes digital forensics, responding to malware or ransomware attacks, and securing networks and IT infrastructures after an intrusion. Their rapid and

effective intervention allows you to minimize the impact of potentially devastating breaches, protecting sensitive data and ensuring business continuity.

- **Network engineers:**
  They play a vital role in managing a company's communications infrastructure. Their expertise is critical in resolving network connectivity and performance issues, especially in situations where the incident directly affects the corporate network. They are responsible for diagnosing and correcting problems related to misconfiguration, service interruptions, or bandwidth saturation. Their job is to ensure that business systems and applications run smoothly, with a focus on the stability and security of networks, including virtual private networks (VPNs) and cloud computing networks.

- **Software developers**:
  They are called upon to intervene when the incident concerns application systems or company software. These professionals possess a deep understanding of the source code of the applications and systems they work on, which allows them to identify bugs, security

vulnerabilities, and inefficiencies. When a critical application stops working properly, developers are able to make a thorough diagnosis, tracing the root causes of the malfunction. They can quickly develop software patches or updates to correct the problem and improve the system's functionality.

- **System Administrators (Sysadmin):**
  System administrators (Sysadmins) play a critical role in managing and maintaining the operating systems that power corporate servers and devices. Their detailed knowledge of configurations, software-hardware interactions, and system resource management makes them indispensable for troubleshooting issues involving the core of the IT infrastructure. When a corporate server crashes or becomes unstable, operating system experts are able to quickly diagnose the cause of the problem, taking action on aspects such as system misconfiguration, resource management, or file system integrity.

Resolution and Recovery

The resolution and recovery phase is the ultimate goal of the incident management process: corrective actions are implemented aimed at restoring regular operations of services as quickly as possible.

This phase, which is crucial for restoring the integrity and availability of business services, requires a strategic and systematic approach to address undesirable events and mitigate their impact on business operations.

Let's take a closer look at the various strategies used to resolve incidents, the importance of service recovery plans, and how to manage temporary solutions to mitigate the impact of incidents on business operations.

Through an in-depth analysis of these subject areas, we try to provide an overall view of best practices and best practices to successfully deal with incidents and ensure business continuity.

Incident resolution strategies

These strategies are designed to address both the immediate manifestations of incidents and their root causes, ensuring comprehensive and effective management of critical situations.

Firstly, immediate corrective actions are an essential component of incident resolution strategies: these actions aim to mitigate the effects of the incident in the shortest possible time, through timely and targeted interventions. This could include, for example, fixing configuration errors, applying security patches, or initiating backup procedures to restore corrupted data. The primary goal of these actions is to ensure that IT services are restored quickly and effectively, while minimizing the impact on business operations.

Incident resolution strategies also include the implementation of long-term preventive measures to prevent the recurrence of similar problems in the future: through this proactive approach, the aim is to investigate the underlying causes of incidents, identifying vulnerabilities and weaknesses in processes.
Through the analysis of the root causes of incidents, it is possible to develop and implement structural or procedural changes aimed at strengthening the resilience of the system and reducing the likelihood of future incidents.

It is important that incident resolution strategies are planned and implemented in a targeted manner considering the specific severity and complexity of each incident.
This requires a thorough analysis of the situation, as well as a thoughtful assessment of the available options.
Adaptability and flexibility of strategies are extremely essential to effectively address the changing and unforeseen challenges that may arise during incident management: only through a holistic and well-thought-out approach can you ensure a complete and lasting resolution

of incidents, thus protecting the integrity and continuity of business operations.

Service Recovery Plans

Service recovery plans are a key element in corporate crisis management, as they precisely outline the procedures, resources and responsibilities necessary to bring interrupted services back to full operation. In an environment where service disruptions can cause significant financial losses, reputational compromise, and diminished customer trust, recovery planning becomes an essential strategic component. These plans not only provide an operational structure for recovery, but also establish a framework for the prevention and mitigation of future risks.

Data recovery and critical asset recovery

A central element of service recovery plans is the recovery of critical data, which is the information asset on which business operations are based. Data recovery can include recovery from off-site backups or secure storage systems, which ensure that up-to-date, intact copies of essential information are protected and available. Data integrity is critical, as errors or corruptions in restored files could further compromise the stability and effectiveness of post-incident operations.

Repair or replacement of hardware and software components

Service recovery plans also include managing the recovery or replacement of damaged hardware and software. It is essential that the technical infrastructure is repaired or replaced quickly to reduce downtime and ensure business continuity. Critical hardware components, such as servers, networking devices, and storage, must be readily available for quick replacement in the event of a failure.

Similarly, software components must be reinstalled, reconfigured, and, if necessary, updated to ensure system stability.

Timely software updates not only ensure business continuity, but also improve safety by preventing similar incidents from happening again. This process requires a well-planned infrastructure that includes the availability of spare hardware and software, as well as properly trained human resources to manage recovery procedures.

Re-enabling system configurations

IT infrastructure recovery is not limited to data recovery and replacement of physical components, but also involves restoring system configurations and operational settings.

Service recovery plans should include specific procedures for reconfiguring networks, restoring security settings, and reactivating critical business applications.

These operations are essential to return the corporate IT environment to its pre-incident operating conditions, avoiding further disruptions.

Without accurate recovery of system configurations, the entire IT ecosystem could remain vulnerable to further operational and security issues.

Importance of Documentation and Regular Testing

A critical aspect of service recovery plans is their accurate and up-to-date documentation. Detailed documentation not only provides operational guidance for personnel involved in recovery activities, but also serves as a training and verification tool to ensure that procedures are carried out correctly in times of crisis.

Clarity in defining responsibilities, necessary resources and operating procedures is essential to ensure a timely and effective response.

However, simple documentation is not enough – recovery plans should be tested regularly to ensure they are viable and up-to-date. Periodic testing allows personnel to familiarize themselves with the procedures, reducing the risk of operational errors in the event of a real incident. In addition, these tests allow you to identify any gaps or areas for improvement in your plans, which can then be optimized to address new risk scenarios. Recovery plans must be constantly reviewed and updated to reflect changes in technologies, infrastructure, and business risks.

Workaround management

These solutions, while temporary, are vital to mitigate the negative impact of the incident on business operations and ensure some business continuity during the resolution process.

It is essential to carefully manage these variances and take precautionary measures to ensure that they do not pose additional security risks or vulnerabilities to the company's IT environment.

Workarounds can take various forms, including implementing alternatives or workarounds to temporarily replace functionality that is compromised or unavailable as a result of the incident.

These solutions may also involve the use of additional resources or backup systems to keep the affected IT services partially operational.

It is crucial that such workarounds are implemented with caution and closely monitored to ensure that they do not cause further complications or security issues.

When implementing and using variances, clear protocols and monitoring procedures should be established to continuously evaluate the effectiveness and safety of such solutions.

This may involve setting deadlines for the use of variances and implementing regular checks to identify any additional risks or negative impacts on business operations.

Once the incident has been completely resolved, the next step will be to remove or replace these temporary solutions with a permanent and permanent solution.

This process requires a smooth transition from temporary solutions to normal IT service operations, ensuring that business operations return to full functionality without compromising system security or integrity.

Closing and Review

The chapter dedicated to the closure and review of incidents represents the last piece of the cycle of managing unwanted events, focusing on the importance of adequately completing the treatment of such events and on the analysis of the experiences gained to improve future processes.

In this final phase, the importance of adopting comprehensive procedures to close incidents accurately and

of using the opportunities provided by the post-incident review to identify strengths and weaknesses in the approach to managing undesirable events is emphasized. We review procedures and best practices for formally closing incidents, emphasizing the importance of comprehensively documenting actions taken, achievements, and any recommendations for future improvements.
This closure phase not only allows for accurate storage of incident-related information, but also provides a crucial opportunity to gather feedback and assessments from stakeholders, thus helping to improve transparency and accountability in dealing with unwanted events.

Another aspect we will focus on is the importance of post-incident review and analysis of lessons learned: this critical evaluation phase allows you to take a deep look at the incident management process, identifying successes achieved and areas where improvements are needed. Through the analysis of the lessons learned, the aim is to identify and implement corrective and preventive actions aimed at strengthening the resilience of the system and reducing the likelihood of future incidents.

Incident Closure Procedures

Incident closure procedures ensure that the incident is properly resolved and that all related issues have been addressed.

These procedures encompass a series of methodical and structured activities that aim to ensure the complete resolution of the incident and the accurate communication of the results to all interested parties.

The closure process begins with the verification of the effective resolution of the incident: this implies an in-depth analysis of the actions taken during the resolution phase, with particular attention to the effectiveness of the countermeasures adopted and the verification of the cessation of the problem.

It is important that this control is rigorous and accurate to avoid the risk of a premature closure of the incident. Subsequently, the closing procedures involve formally closing the support tickets associated with the incident. This step involves recording and documenting all activities performed, resolution times, and feedback collected during the process. Such documentation not only provides a clear track of the actions taken, but is also a valuable source of information for future analysis and review.

Another key component of closure procedures is communicating the outcome of the incident to affected users: it is essential to clearly and comprehensively inform affected users about the status of the resolution, any corrective actions taken, and the preventive measures put in place to avoid future recurrences.

This transparent communication not only helps to restore user trust, but also represents an important gesture of accountability and transparency on the part of the organization.

Finally, closure procedures require confirmation of the complete restoration of the affected services: this process involves further verification of the functionality and reliability of the IT services affected by the incident, ensuring that they have returned to their full operation without compromise or residual impact.

Documentation and feedback

Accurate documentation of incidents and their resolutions not only ensures transparency and traceability of the actions taken, but also represents a valuable repository of knowledge for future operations and the continuous evolution of business processes.

Detailed recording of incident-related information, including details of issues encountered, corrective actions taken, and resources involved, provides a solid foundation for analyzing incident management and identifying areas for improvement.

Comprehensive incident documentation also allows you to capture lessons learned during the resolution process – these lessons not only provide valuable insight into the underlying causes of incidents, but also provide a learning opportunity for the entire organization.

Through a critical analysis of lessons learned, it is possible to identify recurring patterns, identify gaps in existing processes and develop preventive strategies to reduce the likelihood of future incidents.

In addition to documenting the incidents themselves, it is equally crucial to collect feedback from users involved in the incident management process. This feedback provides valuable insight into the user experience during the incident and evaluates the effectiveness of the responses provided. Through careful evaluation of user feedback, strengths and weaknesses can be identified in the incident management process, allowing for continuous improvement of business practices and protocols.

Post-Incident Review and Lessons Learned

The post-incident review provides a critical opportunity to examine in depth the events that led to the incident, identify the underlying causes, and develop strategies to prevent its recurrence.

During this phase, all stakeholders must be involved in order to obtain a complete and accurate view of the events:

- Technical staff
- Business process managers
- The users involved

Post-incident analysis should be conducted in a methodical and detailed manner, with the goal of identifying vulnerabilities in the system, gaps in processes, and potential areas for improvement.

Not only does this process focus on determining the immediate causes of the incident, but it also seeks to pinpoint the deepest roots of the problems, such as design errors, lack of training, or deficiencies in safety controls.

Lessons learned during the post-incident review should be fully and accurately documented: these lessons constitute a valuable repository of knowledge for the organization, providing a solid foundation for future improvements in company processes, procedures, and policies.

Through an in-depth analysis of the lessons learned, it is possible to identify and implement targeted corrective and preventive actions, in order to reduce the risk of future incidents and improve the overall resilience of the organization.

It is important that the lessons learned during the post-incident review are integrated into the organization's continuous improvement cycle. This involves not only implementing immediate corrective actions, but also adapting and evolving business processes in response to the challenges and lessons learned from incident analysis.

Ownership and Monitoring

The chapter dedicated to the ownership and monitoring of incidents represents an in-depth investigation of the concept of responsibility in dealing with undesirable events and emphasizes the importance of constant monitoring to ensure effective incident management in the context of IT services.

Let's take a closer look at the definition of *incident ownership* by exploring the concept of responsibility assigned to specific individuals or teams in incident management.

Such ownership not only implies taking direct responsibility for the resolution process, but also careful oversight and guidance throughout all stages of the incident lifecycle.

Continuous monitoring is another key aspect covered in this chapter. Constant monitoring of IT infrastructures, services, and performance metrics is essential to early spot any anomalies or warning signs that could indicate the presence of an ongoing or imminent incident.

Through active and systematic surveillance, organizations are able to react promptly to undesirable events and implement corrective measures in a timely manner in order to minimize the negative impact on business operations.

We will further explore the importance of internal and external communications during the incident management process: clear and timely communications are crucial to keep all stakeholders informed about the status of incidents, the actions taken, and the expected timelines for resolution. Effective communication not only fosters transparency and trust within the organization, but also helps mitigate uncertainty and anxiety among end-users and other external stakeholders.

Definition of "ownership" of the incident

Ownership of an incident entails a clearly defined and unambiguous responsibility in the complete management of the event's lifecycle, which extends from the identification of the incident to its final resolution and formal closure.
In this context, whoever assumes the role of owner of an incident has the primary task of coordinating all activities related to the management of the incident itself, maintaining constant control over the progress of operations and the resources employed.
The owner's responsibility begins with an accurate and detailed record of the incident. This phase requires rigorous documentation of all relevant information, such as the time of occurrence, the extent of the damage, the resources involved, and the first actions taken. Proper recording not only provides a solid foundation for monitoring the incident, but is also essential for subsequent analysis and the identification of any recurring patterns that may require preventive corrective action.
Continuous monitoring is an essential component of the

ownership process, as it allows you to assess in real time the evolution of the incident and the effectiveness of the measures taken to resolve it: the incident owner must monitor progress with meticulous attention, ensuring that all phases of resolution proceed in a coordinated manner and that there are no unexpected slowdowns or obstacles. Monitoring should not only be limited to the technical resolution of the problem, but must also involve the management of communications, so that all stakeholders receive timely and accurate updates.

Supervision of progress implies the proactive management of resources, both human and technological, involved in the resolution of the incident: the owner must constantly evaluate the effectiveness of the resources available and, if necessary, intervene to optimize processes or request additional specialized skills.

In some cases, you may need to involve external teams or require the use of advanced tools to speed up the resolution process.

The ultimate goal is always to minimize the impact of the incident on business operations and user service, with a focus on reducing downtime and limiting damage.

Effective communication is another crucial aspect of the role of owner.

Throughout the duration of the incident, the owner must

facilitate the continuous exchange of information between the various actors involved, including technical teams, managers, and company stakeholders. This communication process must be structured in such a way as to avoid information gaps or misunderstandings that could compromise the speed or effectiveness of the resolution. The owner's ability to ensure that all necessary decisions are made consciously and at an appropriate time is crucial to maintaining control over the incident and ensuring that it does not get out of hand.

In the context of incident management, the owner must also consider post-incident management, which includes critically reviewing actions taken, identifying root causes, and recommending changes to business or technical processes to prevent similar incidents from occurring in the future.

This review, often formalized in a *post-mortem report*, is a key step in continuously improving incident response and strengthening the organization's operational resilience.

Internal and external communications

Internal and external communications play a key role in ensuring collaboration and transparency during all phases of incident resolution, contributing significantly to the overall success of the critical event management process. Efficient communication management ensures that all stakeholders, internal and external, are adequately informed and able to make decisions based on up-to-date data, thereby minimizing inefficiencies and reducing the negative impact of the incident.

Internally, timely and structured communication between team members and with other business functions involved is critical to ensuring a coordinated and consistent response to incidents.

This internal communication must be proactive, continuous and detailed, including regular updates on the status of the incident, the actions already taken, the problems encountered and the need for any additional resources or specialized skills: an information flow of this type allows all team members to have a clear view of the operational context, reducing the risk of duplication of efforts or uncoordinated interventions, which could aggravate the situation or delay the resolution.

The management of internal communications must also include the use of appropriate tools to facilitate the rapid exchange of information: incident management systems, real-time collaboration platforms and centralized monitoring tools are examples of technological resources that can optimize internal communication.

These tools allow for immediate dissemination of critical information to all stakeholders, ensuring that everyone involved has access to accurate and up-to-date data on the status of the incident.

External communications are also of equally strategic importance, as they involve users, customers, suppliers and other stakeholders who may be directly or indirectly affected by the incident: transparency and clarity in the transmission of this information are essential to preserve the trust of external parties, demonstrating that the organization is aware of the problem, is managing its effects and is actively working to resolve it. This requires that external communications provide accurate details on the impact of the incident, the root causes, the estimated timelines for resolution, and the corrective actions taken. Communications should be tailored to the target audience: for example, more in-depth technical details might be reserved for specific groups of technical users, while a simplified version of the information might be better suited to customers and end users.

A further aspect of external communications concerns the ability to provide practical guidance to users during the incident: in particularly critical situations, users may need to take alternative or temporary measures to continue their operations.

Communicating possible solutions or workarounds accurately and quickly can help minimize the negative impact on users' activities, thus reducing their frustration and potentially preventing further operational or reputational damage.

Such measures may include:

- the use of alternative channels to access the services,
- the redirection of traffic to secondary infrastructures
- the implementation of temporary solutions until the complete resolution of the incident.

External communications are also not limited to just managing the immediate problem, but must include regular updates even after the incident. Once services are restored, it is essential that users are informed of the causes that caused the disruption, the solutions taken, and the preventive actions put in place to prevent similar incidents from occurring in the future.

This post-incident reporting approach not only demonstrates the organization's accountability but also provides an opportunity to further strengthen stakeholder confidence in the organization's ability to manage and resolve complex situations.

Continuous Improvement

The concept of continuous improvement aims to constantly identify areas for improvement and to make changes to increase the efficiency and effectiveness of incident management processes.

We will delve into the importance of analyzing trends and historical data, continuous improvement initiatives, and updating policies and procedures, recognizing these tools as critical to ensuring an increasingly efficient and responsive incident management cycle.

Analyzing trends and historical data allows you to identify patterns, anomalies, and recurring areas of criticality: through a thorough analysis of this data, organizations can gain a clearer understanding of the underlying causes of incidents and opportunities for process optimization.

Continuous improvement initiatives, fueled by data analytics, aim to implement incremental and significant improvements in incident management processes.
This can include optimizing workflows, updating standard operating procedures, and implementing new technologies or tools to improve operational efficiency and incident response.

Constantly updating policies and procedures is essential to ensure that incident management practices are aligned with industry best practices and the evolving needs of the organization.

This process requires a proactive approach to reviewing and adjusting existing policies based on lessons learned from previous incidents and developments in the technological and operational landscape.

Analyzing trends and historical data

Analyzing trends and historical data can help you identify patterns and underlying causes that can influence the frequency and severity of unwanted events.
This analytical process provides organizations with a detailed overview of operational dynamics and the factors contributing to incidents, allowing them to take targeted preventive and corrective measures.

Through the use of sophisticated data analysis tools, companies can examine a wide range of performance metrics, incident frequencies, and other key indicators. This in-depth analysis allows you to identify significant trends and patterns, which can reveal areas of vulnerability or opportunities for improvement in operational processes and IT systems.

Trend analysis could reveal an increase in the frequency of incidents during certain times of the year or in relation to specific business activities: this could suggest the presence of seasonality in problems or the need to strengthen certain processes before critical events.

Similarly, analyzing historical data could highlight correlations between certain types of incidents and certain system configurations or user actions, allowing the organization to take targeted preventive measures. Analyzing trends and historical data provides a solid foundation for identifying continuous improvement initiatives: by identifying the underlying causes of incidents and understanding the factors that contribute to their recurrence, organizations can develop and implement strategies to mitigate future risks and optimize operational efficiency.

Continuous improvement initiatives

Continuous improvement initiatives aim to continuously optimize processes and procedures in order to promote superior operational efficiency and reduce the risk of future undesirable events.

These initiatives span a wide range of proactive activities aimed at identifying and addressing areas of weakness and enhancing strengths in incident management processes. Continuous improvement initiatives include the implementation of new tools and technologies, which could involve the adoption of innovative incident management software, advanced monitoring systems, or more sophisticated data analysis tools.

The introduction of these cutting-edge technologies can improve operational efficiency, allowing for faster identification and resolution of incidents, as well as better prediction and prevention of future anomalies.

In addition, continuous improvement initiatives include reviewing and optimizing existing workflows. This involves critically examining current processes for inefficiencies, delays, or areas of overlap, with the goal of streamlining operations, reducing response times, and improving coordination between teams involved in incident management.

Another important component of continuous improvement initiatives is staff training. Investing in staff training and skills development can improve incident awareness, increase technical proficiency, and foster a culture of accountability and proactivity in handling unwanted events.

It is crucial to actively involve staff and stakeholders in the continuous improvement process: this involvement ensures that initiatives are well received and supported by those who will be directly involved in the implementation of the changes.

It also fosters an organizational culture that values innovation, continuous learning, and adaptation to the changing needs of the operating environment.

Updating policies and procedures

Regularly updating policies and procedures ensures continuous alignment with business goals and industry best practices.

This process requires a periodic and critical review of operational guidelines and protocols to ensure that they are appropriate to the evolving needs of the business and emerging challenges in the technological and regulatory landscape.

Policies and procedures should be reviewed in the light of lessons learned from previous incidents: this involves a detailed analysis of the underlying causes of undesirable events, the responses taken and the results obtained. Incorporating these lessons learned into policies and procedures improves their effectiveness and strengthens the organization's ability to prevent and respond to future incidents more efficiently.

The evolving technological and regulatory landscape requires constant adaptation of policies and procedures:

new technologies may introduce new challenges or opportunities in incident management, while regulatory changes may require compliance requirements and operating procedures to be updated.

Keeping policies and procedures aligned with those changes ensures that the organization remains compliant and ready to effectively handle new challenges as they arise.

Updating policies and procedures ensures that the approach to incident management is always at the forefront and responsive to the needs of the business and the operating environment.
This ongoing process of review and improvement helps ensure that the organization is able to proactively adapt to changing conditions and maintain a high standard of operational resilience and security.

Incidents On-Premise vs Cloud and Hybrid

Incident management takes on different connotations depending on whether it occurs in on-premise, cloud or hybrid environments, where the characteristics of the architectures and the related responsibilities differ significantly.

We explore some of the key distinctions between these

different configurations, focusing on architectural and liability variations, differences in attack surface and security, the importance of regulatory compliance, with particular regard to GDPR, and peculiarities in security management, such as the presence of a DMZ (*Demilitarized Zone*).

In an on-premises environment, IT resources are hosted and managed within the company's physical infrastructure: this scenario requires greater direct control over resources and security, but also requires significant investments in infrastructure and specialized personnel.

Cloud services offer flexibility and scalability, allowing organizations to deploy resources on demand and pay only for what they use, but migrating to the cloud brings new security and compliance challenges as responsibilities are shared between the cloud provider and the user.

Hybrid environments combine on-premises and cloud elements, offering a trade-off between on-premises control and cloud flexibility: this setup presents unique challenges in incident management, as it requires synchronization and consistency between the two environments.

The architectural diversity between these environments directly affects the attack surface and potential threat vectors, requiring a specific assessment of risks and appropriate countermeasures.

The compliance aspect, particularly with regulations such as GDPR, is crucial in all of these environments, but it can be handled differently depending on the configuration adopted.

The presence of a DMZ in on-premises environments can offer additional protection between internal and external networks, while in cloud environments this separation can be implemented through additional access controls and security policies.

Architectures and Responsibilities

The differences between on-premise, cloud, and hybrid architectures are not limited to the simple location of computing resources, but profoundly affect the dynamics of accountability and incident management processes. Each architectural model has specific implications for security, skill distribution, and response capability, requiring tailored approaches to ensure effective incident resolution and operational integrity is maintained.

In on-premises systems, organizations retain full control of the IT infrastructure, which is physically hosted within the company. This model assigns organizations sole responsibility for safety, monitoring, and incident management. Every component of the infrastructure, from networking to the operating system, is under the direct control of internal staff.

In this context, the ability to respond promptly to incidents depends heavily on the availability of qualified technical resources and advanced monitoring tools that allow for timely identification of threats and rapid resolution of critical events. This requires substantial investment not only in security hardware and software, but also in specialized personnel who are trained and up-to-date on the latest technologies and evolving threat landscape.

An additional benefit of on-premises environments is the ability to tailor security measures to the specific needs of the organization, which may not always be possible in cloud environments where control is limited. However, internal management presents significant challenges, including the burden of ensuring continuity of operations and data security, especially in the event of major incidents such as ransomware attacks or infrastructure outages.

In a cloud environment, responsibility for incident management is shared between the customer and the cloud service provider, according to the so-called shared responsibility model. In this model, the provider is generally responsible for the physical security of the infrastructure (including datacenters, physical networks, and virtual machines), while the user is responsible for the security of the applications, data, and configurations they use in the cloud.

This means that while the cloud provider offers robust security measures for the underlying infrastructure, such as firewalls and intrusion prevention systems, the user must implement and manage application-specific controls, such as data encryption, access management, and suspicious activity monitoring. The user must also be well informed about the service level agreement (SLA), which clearly defines the provider's responsibilities in the event of incidents, such as service availability, response times, and mitigation actions.

The ability to collaborate between user and provider becomes essential in the event of an incident. The user must know how to interface quickly with the provider to ensure that all necessary measures are taken in real time, especially when the incident involves infrastructures over which the user has less direct control.

Hybrid environments represent a combination of on-premises and cloud resources, creating a complex setup in which incident management responsibilities are distributed between the company and the cloud provider, often in a variable way depending on the resources involved. This type of architecture offers a trade-off between local control over critical assets and the flexibility of the cloud to handle fluctuating workloads or to take advantage of the scalability and cost-effectiveness offered by cloud services.

Incident management in hybrid environments requires a clear definition of responsibilities for each component of the system. Organizations must establish well-defined processes to ensure that incidents are handled in a coordinated manner between on-premises and cloud-hosted resources. This includes creating protocols that allow response actions to be synchronized between internal teams, which are responsible for on-premises resources, and the cloud provider, which is responsible for remote resources.

The interaction between the two environments increases the complexity of incident management, as a breach or malfunction could impact both architectures.

For example, an incident on an on-premise server could compromise data synchronization with a cloud system, or a cloud service outage could affect critical operations managed locally. To mitigate these risks, you need to implement unified monitoring solutions that allow you to have visibility into the entire IT ecosystem, ensuring that any anomalies are detected and dealt with promptly, regardless of their source.

Attack Surface and Security

The attack surface is the set of vulnerabilities, entry points, and potential weaknesses that can be exploited by malicious actors, internal or external, to compromise the security of a system, network, or infrastructure. It varies significantly depending on the computing environment, which can be on-premise, cloud, or a combination of both. Effective attack surface management requires a structured approach that can be adapted to the specificities of each context.

In on-premises environments, the attack surface is heavily influenced by whether hardware and software resources are entirely under the direct control of the organization. This gives companies a greater level of control over the physical and logical security of infrastructure. However, this autonomy also comes with a higher responsibility for security management, as the company must directly take care of updating and maintaining critical assets. Vulnerabilities can come from a variety of sources, including:

- **Network hardware and devices**:

  Firewalls, routers, servers, and endpoints are vulnerable to attack if they are not properly configured or have vulnerabilities that are not patched. Network devices can be exploited through targeted attacks, such as compromising routers or switches, to gain access to the internal network.

- **Operating systems and local applications**:

  Patch and update management becomes crucial to protect assets from exploits that can exploit known security flaws. Failure to apply critical patches in a timely manner poses a significant risk to system integrity.

Physical access:

In on-premises environments, the risk of unauthorized physical access to infrastructure is something to consider carefully. Internal attacks, for example by employees or contractors with privileged access, pose a threat to the security of critical data and assets.

Managing the attack surface in this context involves not only protecting against digital risks, but also a robust physical defense and a well-defined access control policy, with the integration of intrusion monitoring and detection systems.

In cloud environments, the attack surface is influenced by the security policies of the cloud service provider and the configurations adopted by the user. The shared responsibility model requires the vendor to be responsible for securing the cloud infrastructure (datacenters, hardware, and networks) and applying updates and patches at the infrastructure level. However, managing the security of applications, configurations, and data remains the responsibility of the user. Key areas of vulnerability include:

- **Incorrect configurations**:
  One of the biggest risks in cloud environments comes from misconfigurations or permissive resource configurations, which can expose sensitive data to the internet or unauthorized users. These configurations can be leveraged for unauthorized access to storage buckets, databases, or virtual machines.

- **DDoS attacks (Distributed Denial of Service)**: the cloud infrastructure, being accessible via the Internet, is exposed to attempts to overload the system through DDoS attacks. However, cloud providers typically offer advanced DDoS mitigation services that monitor and filter traffic to protect customers from these types of threats.

Threats related to unauthorized access: Using compromised or insufficiently protected credentials (such as weak passwords) can allow attackers to gain access to cloud resources. It is therefore critical to implement strong authentication mechanisms, such as multi-factor authentication (MFA), to reduce the risk of compromise.

Cloud service providers often implement advanced security measures to protect the infrastructure and services they provide. These include continuous network monitoring, intrusion prevention systems (IPS), encryption of data both in transit and at rest, and tools for detecting anomalous behavior that could indicate attack attempts.
However, it's critical that users properly configure these tools and constantly monitor the resources and data they manage in the cloud.

A critical vulnerability in the cloud environment involves exposed APIs. Cloud-based applications often use APIs to communicate with other services or to enable third-party integration. Unsecured or misconfigured APIs can provide direct access for attackers, allowing them to bypass security mechanisms and manipulate data or systems.

Hybrid environments, which combine on-premises and cloud resources, introduce additional complexity into managing security and attack surface. In these scenarios, the attack surface extends to both on-premises infrastructure, which must be protected with traditional measures, and cloud infrastructure, which requires a more dynamic and scalable approach to security. The risk lies in maintaining consistency in security policies between the two environments and ensuring that any vulnerabilities in one of them do not result in an access point for attacks that could compromise the entire infrastructure.

For example, an attacker who exploits a vulnerability on an on-premises system could use it to gain access to resources in the cloud, if there are not sufficient security barriers between the two infrastructures. In addition, connectivity solutions that connect the two environments, such as virtual private networks (VPNs) or dedicated connections, represent potential points of vulnerability if not properly configured and secured.

In any context – on-premises, cloud or hybrid – attack surface management requires a holistic and proactive approach to security. It is essential for organizations to carry out continuous assessments of their assets and potential vulnerabilities, taking into account factors such as evolving threats and changes in IT architecture.
Vulnerability assessment and penetration testing tools can be used to identify and mitigate vulnerabilities before they can be exploited by attackers.
Network segmentation is another key strategy to reduce the attack surface. By separating different network segments and restricting access permissions based on operational needs, you can reduce the risk of a breach in one part of the infrastructure spreading to other critical areas.
In addition, staff training plays a vital role. Even the best security technology can be ineffective if people aren't properly trained to recognize threats like phishing, manage security configurations, and follow best practices for using credentials and logins.

Compliance and GDPR

Regulatory compliance, with particular reference to the GDPR (General Data Protection Regulation), is a crucial element in incident management, as it aims to safeguard the protection of personal data and the privacy of individuals, requiring organizations to take specific measures to ensure that sensitive data is processed securely and transparently. This regulation applies to all organizations that process European citizens' data, regardless of their geographical location, and has a significant impact on both on-premise and cloud environments, which require different approaches to ensure compliance.

In on-premises environments, the increased direct control over the IT infrastructure can make it easier to comply with regulations as resources and data remain physically within the company. This allows organizations to implement and manage security measures on their own, such as access control, encryption of sensitive data, and continuous monitoring of activities.

However, such control also requires a significant investment in terms of human, financial and technological resources to maintain a high level of compliance, especially with regard to the processing, storage and secure disposal of personal data.

In cloud environments, the situation becomes more complex as responsibility for data management is shared between the customer and the cloud provider. Organizations must ensure that the cloud provider complies with the security and privacy requirements of the GDPR, particularly regarding data localization and how data is managed and protected. Data processed in cloud infrastructures must be subject to strict controls that ensure that it is not transferred to countries outside the European Economic Area (EEA) without the appropriate legal safeguards, such as standard contractual clauses approved by the European Commission or specific data protection certifications.

Another key aspect in cloud environments is the evaluation of the SLA (Service Level Agreement) and DPAs (Data Processing Agreements) stipulated with service providers. Such contracts must clearly specify each party's responsibilities for the management and protection of personal data, including the technical and organizational measures taken to prevent unauthorized access, loss or breach of data.

Providers must also ensure that data is processed in accordance with the principles of minimization and restriction of processing, which are fundamental in the GDPR.

In the context of incident management, GDPR compliance is particularly relevant in the event of a data breach involving personal data. According to Article 33 of the GDPR, organizations are obliged to notify the competent supervisory authority within 72 hours of discovering the fact of an incident involving a personal data breach, unless it can be demonstrated that the breach does not result in risks to the rights and freedoms of natural persons. In addition, if the breach may entail a high risk for the data subjects, they must be informed in a clear and understandable manner in good time.

Proactive incident management therefore becomes essential to ensure a timely and compliant response. Organizations must have well-defined operating procedures in place to quickly identify incidents, assess their severity, and make quick decisions on corrective measures to be taken. These procedures include not only the technical management of the incident, but also the detailed documentation of each step of the process, from causes to resolution, up to the implementation of preventive measures to avoid the recurrence of the event.

It is also essential that each breach event undergoes a thorough Root Cause Analysis (RCA) to understand the circumstances that led to the incident and improve security and compliance practices. The adoption of solutions such as security information and event management (SIEM) and automated incident response tools can facilitate the collection and analysis of information related to events, facilitating effective management and timely reporting of incidents to authorities.

An additional crucial point in ensuring compliance is the continuous control and monitoring of the cloud service providers with which the company collaborates. Organizations must ensure that these providers comply with the necessary technical and organizational measures to protect the personal data processed, including the adoption of advanced security protocols, data encryption, and active threat monitoring.

Contractual agreements must clearly state that suppliers are required to promptly inform the customer organization in the event of breaches involving personal data, providing all the information necessary for a rapid response and compliance with regulatory requirements. These agreements may also include clauses requiring suppliers to undergo periodic security audits and maintain compliance certifications such as ISO/IEC 27001, which attest to compliance with international information security management standards.

DMZ and Security Differences

The Demilitarized Zone (DMZ), in on-premises environments, represents a central component in the security architecture, providing a physical and logical separation between internal networks and untrusted external networks, such as the internet. This concept, developed to protect critical business assets, allows only selected services to be exposed to the public, such as web or mail servers, while keeping internal systems protected behind additional layers of security. The DMZ thus acts as a defensive barrier that minimizes the risk of compromise of internal networks in the event of breaches by external actors.

Implementing a DMZ in on-premise environments is usually supported by multiple firewalls, one placed between the external network and the DMZ, and another between the DMZ and the internal network. This additional layer of security allows for strict control of network traffic, where only authorized and monitored connections can pass to and from the DMZ. Organizations can also configure granular access policies that determine which services or applications are publicly accessible, mitigating the risk that attacks from outside can propagate within the network. Among the main advantages offered by the DMZ is the ability to manage publicly accessible services (such as web servers, DNS, FTP servers) separately from critical internal resources. This way, an attacker who manages to compromise one in the DMZ will not be able to easily reach the internal systems, as additional layers of defense will hinder him. This network segmentation model thus reduces the attack surface, making it more difficult for an attacker to access sensitive data or critical infrastructure.

In the cloud environment, the traditional concept of DMZ is often less relevant or implemented differently. This is due to the peculiarities of cloud infrastructure and the advanced security strategies that service providers provide. Unlike on-premises environments, where network protection is heavily dependent on physical segmentation and traffic control through hardware firewalls, in the cloud, security is more often managed through software-defined networks (SDN), resource virtualization, and policy-based access controls. In a cloud environment, in fact, vendors implement security models that can integrate functionalities similar to those of a DMZ, but through virtualized mechanisms and segmented logical networks. For example, through the use of virtual private clouds (VPCs) or isolated subnets, organizations can isolate network segments and apply software-level routing rules and firewalls to control traffic between cloud resources and external or internal networks. Encrypting data in transit and at rest is another critical layer of protection, ensuring that even if an attack manages to break through virtual barriers, your information remains protected.

In addition, cloud service providers implement advanced measures such as continuous monitoring, intrusion detection, and DDoS protection on a global scale, making some of the traditional physical defenses of the DMZ less relevant or duplicative. These tools enable proactive threat control without the need for dedicated physical facilities, such as the DMZ. However, cloud models require companies to carefully define their access rules and security policies to avoid misconfigurations, which could expose sensitive resources to external threats.

Enterprises considering migrating their infrastructures between on-premises and cloud environments must carefully consider the differences between the security models offered by each context. In an on-premise environment, having a DMZ provides greater direct control, but it also means that security systems are continuously managed and constantly updated. In contrast, in the cloud, security is managed at the software and policy level, with the advantage of being able to take advantage of the continuous updates and advanced measures provided by the provider. However, this requires a clear understanding of shared responsibilities and proper implementation of security configurations.

Businesses should consider whether adopting a hybrid architecture, combining on-premises elements with cloud services, might be a better fit for their security needs. In such a setup, it might be useful to maintain a DMZ to protect critical internal assets, while leveraging the scalable solutions and advanced security measures offered by cloud providers for less sensitive or highly dynamic applications.

Problem Management: a use case

The management and resolution of one or more incidents can generate a "Problem".

Below we see what a Problem is and an example of a management process and its resolution.

Definition and Purpose of Problem Management:

Problem Management is a process aimed at identifying the root causes of incidents in order to prevent their recurrence. This process aims to minimize the impact and frequency of incidents, improve the quality of service and strengthen the overall management of IT services.

Often, the cause is unknown at the time the problem is identified, and Problem Management is responsible for leading further investigations to determine the root cause and monitor actions to resolve it. It is a goal-oriented process that aims to reduce the impact of incidents on the organization, improve the overall health of IT services – including availability, reduce downtime, and increase customer satisfaction.

Each problem is assigned to a Problem Owner, usually the Problem Manager himself. They are responsible for coordinating the resolution of the problem from start to finish in a timely and effective manner. They can monitor various activities by opening a Task.

The task can be about Analysis, Root Cause Analysis, Implementation, or a general topic. The Problem Task

Owner is responsible for carrying out the investigation by performing the task assigned by the Problem Owner.

Problem Management's stakeholders

Each problem is assigned to a Problem Owner, usually the Problem Manager himself. They are responsible for coordinating the resolution of the problem from start to finish in a timely and effective manner. They can monitor various activities by opening a Task. The task can concern the phases of Assess, Root Cause Analysis, Fix implementation or a general topic.

The Problem Task Owner is responsible for carrying out the investigation by performing the task assigned by the Problem Owner.

Problem Management Process

The Problem Management process includes diagnosis, resolution and implementation of solutions, often through Change Management. This process relies on the use of ITSM tools (e.g.: ServiceNow) to track and manage issues efficiently. The problem goes through phases such as *Draft, Assess, Root Cause Analysis, Fix Implementation, Resolved,* and *Closed,* each with specific actions and criteria for moving to the next phase.

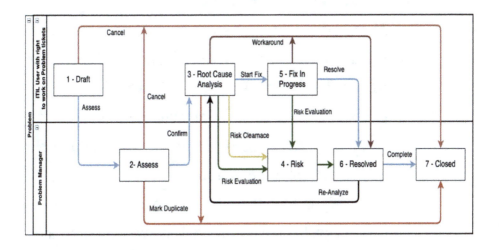

- **DRAFT:**

  In this first phase, the presence of a new case is reported in the tool dedicated to problem management and the available information is entered with any references to incidents generated by the problem

- **ASSESS:**

  In this phase, the Problem Management team evaluates the request for the new problem record. If everything is in place, a Problem Manager approves the ticket, moves it to the next stage - Root Cause Analysis, and opens tasks to the relevant stakeholders.

- **ROOT CAUSE ANALYSIS:**

  At this stage, the problem is officially approved. Here the tasks necessary for the relevant stakeholders for root cause analysis are opened. They define the root cause of the problem and an action plan to solve it definitively. At this stage, there are several options in addition to solving the problem:

  o If the root cause cannot be identified (in the worst case) and there is no workaround, the Problem Manager clicks the button to open a Risk task to the Application Owner.

  o If the root cause is identified, but the solution cannot be implemented due to lack of budget/resources or will be executed within a project, the Problem Manager will open a Risk task to the Application Owner.

  o If the root cause is identified, but the actions taken are not the most appropriate, then the Problem Manager compiles a new Primary Known Error article for the Known Error Database. Note that the "Workaround" resolution code can be decided later, in the "Fix in Progress" phase, and is not a phase like Risk Assessment and Risk Closure.

In the best case (and this is generally the case), the root cause is identified and actions can be taken. In that case, the problem manager enters a failure and sub-failure code based on the root cause and clicks to move the ticket to the next step: Fix Implementation.

- **FIX IMPLEMENTATION:**

  In this phase, the Problem Manager opens a task for each action. The due date is agreed with the Problem Task Owner. When the task is closed with an analysis/implementation, the Problem Manager writes a closing note about the problem. If there is a workaround, then the Problem Manager performs the actions described in the previous step. Note that when a problem is resolved, it does not mean that it is closed.

RESOLVED:

During this phase, all problem managers meet for an internal meeting once a week to review Resolved tickets and decide whether to close them. If they realize that something is missing, the problem will return to the Root Cause Analysis. Otherwise, if they decide to close it, the ticket will be QA and the issue will be moved to the Closed phase.

Here, there is another crucial step if the resolution code is one of them: *Workaround*, *Risk Assessment* or *Risk Closure*. If the problem is solved with one of these codes, then Problem Managers can track these problems internally and start another process: Potential Bug Management.

- **CLOSED:**

  At this final stage, no further action can be taken. Once an issue is closed, it cannot be reopened. Here, we only see the information we entered previously and cannot make changes.

Key concepts

Here are some of the main concepts examined in the field of Incident Management:

1. **Incident management**:
    The process for the timely management of events that can compromise IT services, including the recording, analysis, and resolution of incidents.

2. **ITIL Framework**:
    A consolidated body of best practices for IT service design and management, including the process for

incident management.

3. **COBIT Framework**:
    Framework for aligning business goals with IT
    operations, including control and governance of
    activities, including incident management.

4. **Incident log**:
    Detailed documentation regarding incidents,
    including the time, date, areas involved, and
    symptoms.

5. **Underlying Cause Analysis**:
    Identification of the root causes of incidents, beyond
    the visible effects.

6. **Incident classification and prioritization**:
    Assigning urgency and severity to incidents for
    resource allocation.

7. **Incident resolution**:
    The process of restoring normal operations of IT
    services, including the implementation of
    workarounds and corrective actions.

8. **Preparation and Prevention:**
    Fundamental actions to deal with unforeseen events.
    Preparedness involves putting resources, processes,
    and personnel in place to address critical situations,

while prevention aims to reduce the risk of incidents through proactively identifying sources of risk and implementing countermeasures.

9. **Identification of warning signs:** Early indications of potential problems or anomalies in IT systems and services, requiring immediate attention and timely response to avoid unintended consequences.

10. **Implementing preventative measures:** Proactive actions to reduce the likelihood of incidents and mitigate their impact, which include implementing security patches, verifying and updating data backup and recovery processes, training staff, and integrating preventative measures into the company culture.

11. **Incident detection:** Early identification of anomalies or deviations from normal operations in the organization's systems and networks through performance monitoring, analysis of event logs, and implementation of automated anomaly detection systems.

12. **Incident reporting:** Quickly and accurately communicate an incident to the team responsible for managing it through formal,

structured systems, such as self-service portals, dedicated phone lines, and incident management software.

13. **Incident detection processes:**
Methods and procedures designed to detect anomalies or outages in systems and networks at an early stage, including monitoring performance, analyzing event logs, and implementing automated anomaly detection systems.

14. **Reporting and communication systems:**
Channels and tools through which users and IT staff can promptly report and communicate about unwanted events and their resolutions, such as self-service portals, dedicated phone lines, and incident management software.

15. **Role of staff in reporting:**
Active involvement of staff in the identification and timely reporting of incidents, through awareness, training and promotion of a corporate culture that values and rewards incident reporting.

16. **Incident classification:**
The process of assessing the severity and urgency of each event based on defined criteria, such as the

impact on business operations, technical complexity and criticality of the services involved.

17. **Incident prioritization:**

A process for allocating resources efficiently, based on analyzing the severity, urgency, and impact of incidents on business operations, ensuring that the most critical incidents are addressed as quickly as possible.

18. **Incident Root Cause Analysis:**

Methodical process of identifying the roots of incidents, including both technical and procedural aspects, in order to prevent their recurrence.

19. **Use of diagnostic tools:**

Use of specialized software to monitor system performance, analyze system logs, and trace networks to support the identification and resolution of incidents.

20. **Resolution and recovery phase:**

The ultimate goal of the incident management process, during which corrective actions are implemented to restore regular service operations as quickly as possible.

21. **Incident resolution strategies:**
Planned and systematic approaches to dealing with incidents, including immediate actions, long-term preventive measures, and adaptive planning to ensure a comprehensive and lasting resolution.

22. **Service Recovery Plans:**
Documented and tested procedures for restoring business services to full functionality after an outage, including data recovery, repair of critical assets, and reactivation of system configurations.

23. **Variance Management:** Implementing interim measures to mitigate the impact of incidents on business operations, with a focus on security and effectiveness, and with a smooth transition to permanent solutions.

24. **Incident Closure: Final**
stage of the incident management cycle, which focuses on the proper completion of incident handling, including detailed documentation of actions taken and transparent communication to Impacted users.

25. **Post-Incident Review and Lessons Learned:**
Critical evaluation conducted after incident resolution

to identify underlying causes and develop future preventive strategies, involving all stakeholders and thoroughly documenting lessons learned for future improvements.

26. **Incident Closure Procedures:**
A series of structured activities to ensure that incidents are fully resolved and outcomes are accurately communicated, including verifying the effectiveness of countermeasures, closing support tickets, and confirming that affected services have been fully restored.

27. **Documentation and feedback:**
Detailed recording of information related to incidents and their resolutions, along with the collection of feedback from the users involved to identify strengths and weaknesses in incident management processes and enable continuous improvement.

28. **Architectural Responsibilities:**
Incident management varies between on-premises, cloud, and hybrid environments due to differences in architectures and responsibilities. In on-premises systems, the organization manages everything in-house, while in the cloud environment, responsibility is shared with the provider.

29. **Security and Attack Surface:**
   Cybersecurity depends on the attack surface, which is different between on-premises and cloud. It requires continuous risk assessment and the implementation of appropriate measures to protect assets and data.

30. **Regulatory Compliance:**
   Incident management must comply with regulations such as GDPR. Companies must align their procedures with regulatory requirements and ensure that cloud providers comply with security and privacy standards.

31. **Role of the DMZ:**
   The DMZ is critical for security in on-premises environments, but in cloud contexts, it can be replaced by integrated security solutions. Companies must carefully evaluate these differences when designing their approaches to incident management.

32. **Problem Management:**
   It is a process aimed at identifying the root causes of incidents to prevent their recurrence, improving the quality of service and strengthening the overall management of IT services.

33. **Problem Owner Responsibilities:**

Each problem is assigned to a Problem Owner, who is responsible for its coordinated and timely resolution.

34. **Problem Management Process:**

Roles:

- Problem Manager,
- Task Owner
- Stakeholders who contribute to the analysis and resolution of the problem.

It includes the steps of:

Draft:

Report the problem and enter the available information.

Assess:

Evaluation of the problem and opening of tasks for root cause analysis.

Root Cause Analysis:

Identification of root causes and definition of an action plan.

Fix Implementation:

Implementation of solutions and closure of

related tasks.

Resolved:

Review of resolved issues and decision on closure.

Closed:

Permanent closure of the problem without the possibility of reopening.

www.ingramcontent.com/pod-product-compliance
Lightning Source LLC
LaVergne TN
LVHW051737050326
832903LV00023B/970